CRIES ⌒⎺

IRISH C⌄

PAUL DURCAN was born in Mayo parents, and studied arch. ⎯⎯⎯ ⎯⎯ ⎯⎯⎯tory at Univeristy College Cork. His first book, *Endsville* (with Brian Lynch), appeared in 1967, and has been followed by 17 others, including *O Westport in the Light of Asia Minor* (1975); *Teresa's Bar* (1976); *Sam's Cross* (1978); *Jesus, Break His Fall* (1980); *The Selected Paul Durcan* (edited by Edna Longley, Poetry Ireland Choice, 1982); *Jumping the Train Tracks with Angela* (1983); *The Berlin Wall Café* (Poetry Book Society Choice, 1985); *Going Home to Russia* (1987); *Daddy, Daddy* (Winner of the Whitbread Award for Poetry, 1990); *Crazy about Women* (1991); *A Snail in My Prime: New and Selected Poems* (1993); *Give Me Your Hand* (1994); the long poem *Christmas Day* (1996); and *Greetings To Our Friends in Brazil* (1999). Apart from Britain and Ireland, where he reads regularly, he has read in the former Yugoslavia, the former Soviet Union, the USA, Canada, Holland, France, Italy, Luxembourg, Belgium, New Zealand, Israel, Germany, Brazil, Portugal, Catalonia, Austria, the Czech Republic, Japan, Sweden, and Australia. ⎯⎯ he received a Cholmondeley Award for poetry. ⌐ ⎯⎯member of Aosdána and lives in Dublin.

Paul Durcan

CRIES OF AN
IRISH CAVEMAN

THE HARVILL PRESS
LONDON

First published in Great Britain in 2001 by
The Harvill Press
2 Aztec Row, Berners Road
London N1 0PW

www.harvill.com

1 3 5 7 9 8 6 4 2

© Paul Durcan, 2001

Paul Durcan asserts the moral right to be
identified as the author of this work

A CIP catalogue record for this title is
available from the British Library

ISBN 1 86046 909 4 (hbk)
ISBN 1 86046 910 8 (pbk)

Designed and typeset in Bembo at
Libanus Press, Marlborough, Wiltshire

Printed and bound in Great Britain by Butler & Tanner Ltd
at Selwood Printing, Burgess Hill

TO
COLM TÓIBÍN

The King of Seals

ACKNOWLEDGEMENTS

Versions of nine of these poems appeared in *Eureka Street* (Melbourne), *A Festschrift for Theo Dorgan*, the *Irish Review*, the *Irish Times*, the *London Review of Books*, the *Sunday Independent*, and *The Shop*.

For shelter and support, advice and many kindnesses, my warmest thanks to Vi McDowell, Mary and Seamus Walsh, Kathleen McCracken, Brian and Mary Kennedy, Clara Mason, Carol Davidson, Matt Foley, Gerard and Louella Windsor, Monica and Ernie Lack, Mary Gallivan, Mary Hoban, Bill and Pippa Swainson, Masazumi Toraiwa, Futoshi Sakauchi, Catriona Crowe, Patrick O'Brien, Susan Kellett, Sarah Durcan, Mark Joyce, Síabhra Durcan and Blaise Drummond. I am glad to record again my gratitude to the Achill Island Heinrich Böll Committee and to Mr Michael Carr.

CONTENTS

Ecology. Folks use that term for everything but what it means: who's eating who.

Arctic Blue

PART ONE

GIVE HIM BONDI

Give Him Bondi

Gerard inquires: "Is there anything you'd like to do
On your last day in Sydney?"
I reply: "I'd like to go to Bondi Beach."
Too cautious to confess:
I'd like to swim at Bondi Beach.
Cautious not for fear of drowning in the sea
(I have been swimming since aged seven –
I've never thought of myself drowning –
Unseen, only other people drown)
But for fear of drowning in my own mortification –
An off-white northman in a sea of bronze
    loin-clothed men
With their bronze loin-clothed women.

As I step down onto the quartz sand of Bondi
I have to step around a young, topless virgin
Lying flat out on her back, eyes shut,
Each breast strewn askew her chest
Like a cone of cream gimleted with a currant
In a shock of its own slack:
Primeval Still Life awaiting the two Chardins,
Teilhard, Jean-Baptiste.

Will she one day
At the age of twenty-two
Not knowing she is not alone
With her infant twins in her arms

Commit suicide
On the newly carpeted staircase
Of her showcase home?
Please God open her closed eyes.

In our black slacks and long-sleeved white shirts
Gerard and I tip-toe up and down Bondi Beach
Like two corkscrewed, avid seminarians
On a day trip to the seaside.
Only that I, in a spasm of morning optimism,
Instead of underpants donned swimming briefs.
I feel – Gerard must also feel –
Estranged from our surroundings;
Teetering loners
Amid flocks of lovers,
Boys and girls
Skating precipices of surf.

In wistful exuberance resuscitating lives
Of priests, nuns, writers we have known –
Solvitur ambulando –
We promenade for an hour before
Gerard cries: "It's nearly time to go."
I am booked to recite to the pupils of his old school –
Robert Hughes's old school, too –
And Mick Scott's and Charlie Fraser's –
St Ignatius's at Riverview in North Sydney.
I gasp: "To hell with it – this is idiocy:
To be standing here at Bondi, not swimming."

I yank down my trousers to expose black briefs –
Too brief, really –
Body-Glory briefs –
And Gerard coughs, smiles, splutters:

"Well played, old chap –
Swim between the flags."
He'll stand guard over my little cache of manhood:
My wristwatch – my twentieth-century tag;
My white shirt folded in a sandwich;
My black slacks curled up in a chaste ball;
My black nylon socks twinned back to back;
My black leather slip-ons with fake gold studs.

I tumble out into the shallows where maybe twenty-five
Youths and maidens gay frolic
And I chin-dive and become a boy again –
A curly-headed blue-eyed fourteen year old
Leaping and whooping in the surf,
Romping into the rollers,
Somersaulting into the dumpers,
A surf-flirt in my element,
In the spray of the foliage of the sea.
Gerard patrols on the fringes of the foam
With his pants rolled up, snapping me
With a disposable *Instamatic* I've handed him.

I essay a breaststroke, but desist –
Being unfit, overweight, dead-beat.
Yesterday I flew in from Ayers Rock;
The day before alone in the low 30s
Humping five litres of water,
I trekked five miles in the Olgas.
Again I strike out, this time with an overarm
But after six or seven strokes flail up against
A barrage of exhaustion.
I spin over self-cossetingly on my spine,
My pudgy vertebrae,
And float, watching my toes:

Inspecting them
Strutting their stuff
On a catwalk of silver faucets,
Toenails pared and gleaming,
Their parings littering
A hotel bathroom floor
In the Northern Territory;
All ten toes of mine present and correct,
Pristine, pink, erect, perky,
Bouncing on a trampoline
Such is the buoyancy of Bondi.

This is my Theory of Floating
Which has served me well,
My Theory of Daydreaming.
If one may speak well of oneself
I may say I have not craved
Conquest or complacency
But exclusively
The existence of existence,
The survival of survival,
The dreaming of the day.
I did not climb Ayers Rock,
Not out of an excess of virtue
But out of a modicum of attention
To the signposts of the local people:
Please do not climb our sacred mountain.
It would have been a sin
Against the genetics
Of all the chromosomes of ethics
To have climbed Ayers Rock.

To float is to be on the whale's back.
Gurgling to myself:
There she blows!
Only three weeks ago
In the company of Mary Clare Power
And Nicholas Shakespeare
On a motorboat off Fraser Island
In Queensland
From fifty yards away
I saw two humpback whales
Steeplechasing the waves, courting;
Rising up, cresting, plunging;
Flaunting their tattooed tails.
Toe-gazing, I go on chatting to myself:
Amn't I a humpback too?
Mother shrieking at me: "Straighten up
Or you'll get curvature of the spine
And you'll be a humpback!"
She meant the Hunchback of Notre Dame.
Guy de Maupassant
Was *her* mother's idol.
Why did *my* mother eat me?
Her mother minded me.
In my prime I could scoff
Back in one gulp
15,000 gallons of salt water
While continuing to speak
Ten to the dozen
About anything under the sun.
Never mind, this day is Elysium!
Alone to own and range
The bush of the sea.
How fortunate I am

Who in spite of all my loss and failure –
All my defeats quadrupling daily –
I find myself here floating at Bondi Beach –
A little, pale saffron, five-and-a-half dollar boomerang
In a black penis-purse.
I flip over my gaze upon the hard blue sky.

But I must not keep Gerard waiting.
Time to swim ashore, go on
With life's obligation.
I flop over on my belly to swim
To see that I am twice as far out
As I should be! Pulled out to sea
While floating! Out of sight
Of the flags! But I'm an old hand
At swimming. Didn't Uncle Mick
Teach all of us to swim
At the age of seven
Off the famine pier
At Enniscrone of the Seaweed Baths?
Out of our depth
On the deep, steep steps
And not, not, not
To be afraid?
By God he did!
I strike out for home.
Only to find myself swimming backwards!
Christ O Lord the sea
Is kidnapping me!
Like that man in the back lane
When I was nine
On my way home from school!
He asked me to climb over a wall

With him and I did. No!
I decline to believe it! No!
             I go
Into denial!
             Stop, sea, stop!
Into hysteria!
             Stop it, stop it!
O save me, save me!
             No! No!
O God, O God!
             O save me, save me.
Of what use be these now –
All thy litanies of ejaculations?
All these cries aeons ago
Airbrushed into extinction.

Pounding forwards I am surging backwards.
Instead of me catching the waves,
The waves are dumping me backwards!
I who presume myself a porpoise
With fifty years of Floating Theory
Chalked up on my flippers
Am now a mouse being toyed with
By the tom-cat of the sea!
In this drifting micromoment
The stopwatch stops:
I behold my death eyeball me
Like a sadistic schoolmaster
Cornering me at the blackboard.

I wave, but no one sees me
And, as I wave, I begin to sink.
I'm being eaten alive.

Save me, O Christ, save me!
Your what? Your own death?
Your own end? Your own oblivion?
Death by drowning?
                    The fury of it!
The remorseless deep closing o'er your head!
Alone, alone, all, all alone!
Within seconds, to be but a swab –
A trace in water –
That scarcely decipherable but tell-tale trace
In the sea after a substance has sunk.
Fear frying your bones.
I thought I had known fear –
Oceans of fear – but I had not:
Not until now
This moment of 100-carat fear;
My body incapable of coping
But my psyche clear with fear
Not muddled or mesmerised,
But clarifed – a seer
Of the final second, seeing
The sea about to snatch,
Suck, swallow me.

The sea! Oh, the sea!
That stunning, wholly together She –
The one with her Mountain Passes
In all the right places.
You've flirted with her all your life
Having it both ways as always;
Your wife your mistress not your wife;
Your mistress your wife not your mistress;

Solitude your company;
Being mortal claiming immortality;
Every single time without exception
That the air hostess models the life jacket
You insouciantly ignore her,
Flaunting yourself a superior stoic
Who plumbs the secret of the voyage.
Voyager your voyage about to end
Faster than an airliner plummeting
How goes your voyaging?

Why are you standing in water
Out of your depth dying?
Far from your own bed?
Naught now between your legs
But disdainful water?
Being buried alive?
Dying, Durcan, dying
In your own standing?
Hanging on by one hand
From the sky's yardarm
About to plop
Down into Davy Jones's locker?
Where be your swashbuckling now?
Your hip-hop-hip mating?
Your waistcoated machismo?
Where be all your cheek-to-cheek glowing?
Your eyebrow-to-eyebrow acrobatics?
Where be all your toe-to-toe conniving?
You are being struck down,
Having glowed, having connived.
Neither being seen nor being heard

But tomorrow in a scrap of newscasting
On ABC:
"Irish poet trapped in rips,
Washed up between the Heads
Of Sydney Harbour."

Ocean – compleat ocean – clenches me
In its JCB claws,
Hissing at me that this time there'll be no pause
And my brains gape down upon my own terror.
In the vice of drowning I know
I have no power, my fate
Decided, all I can
Be said to be doing is lingering;
Out of my depth, flailing
Legs, arms, caterwauling
In my kitty
And meekly screaming – I am lingering;
Fresh blows the breeze from off the bow;
My Irish boy, where lingerest thou?
This fling in which you're lingering
Will last but seconds and after
You will be but a thing
Flung against the automatic sliding doors
Of the sea's casino.
My father and mother
Each a wowser
Resenting one another,
Resented me
Because I was a bother.
How so much better
It would have been

Not to have given birth
To such a bother.
All presumption walloped o'er the horizon,
All my naïveté, all my toxic pride,
All my vanity, all my conceit.
There is nothing I can do – I realise –
Except shout, cry, whimper.
In the cot of the sea,
On the rails of the waves
I bang my little knuckles.
The sea seethes:
Paul Durcan, you are
The epitome of futility.

I cry out "Help! Help!"
But no one hears me.
A cry? I –
Did I ever reply
To a cry?
A cry of a tiny, frail Scotsman
In a damp basement bedsit
In Buckingham Palace Road
Choking on his own loneliness?
Aye! A cry!
Nobody hears me, the dead man!
I cry out again with all my ego.
The about-to-be overtaken sprinter
At the finishing line,
Lunging one last futile fingertipsbreadth.
The ocean is the mighty woman
You have hunted all your life.
But now that she has got you

In the palm of her hand –
In her thimble of no reprieve! –
You are crying out "Help"!
She is moulding her knuckles around you.
You are her prey.
This is the yarn you will not live to spin,
The blackest yarn,
A ground swell is spinning out your life
At once slowly, speedily –
A ground swell no longer a cliché
But a mother of death!
You are a puppet out of your depth
And your legs are diced dancers
Dangling from deadwood,
Thrashing in their throes
Out of sight slipping.
The sea is a headless goddess
All flesh sans eyes sans mouth.
Paul Durcan, this is one lady
Through whose eyes and mouth,
Through whose free looks
You will not talk your way.

HELP!
My teensy-weensy voicette fetches
Over the uncut surf and the sealed ocean
To two young men who shout back –
Their seal heads bobbing a quarter-mile off –
Something like "Hold on! Hold on!"
And blubbering I pant for breath
As my head slides beneath the waves,
My shoulders caving in,
My paunch of guts dragging me down,

My kidneys wincing,
My crimson ankles skipping,
My snow-white fetlocks like faulty pistons
Halting for the last time.

I can hear myself sobbing "O God, O God!"
Floating downwards with every surge;
Hurtling upwards with every heave.
"O Christ, I don't want to die!
After all that church-going and hymn-singing
This is not the only life I know
But it's the only life I want!
O God O God I want to live!"
They clutch me round the neck
And flail and thrash to lug me shorewards.
A third joins them – an off-duty lifeguard
Called Brian who happens to be doing
A stint of training – but the breaking rollers
At each crash uppercut me.
Each other roller clubs me on the head.
Not once of course, but again again
Clubbing, clubbing, clubbing,
Such stuffing as is in me goes limp.
My rescuers scream: "Keep your lips tight shut!"
As each wave crashes I writhe for consciousness –
A newborn baby pawing air;
My lungs spewing up bladders of salt water –
The rash smart sloggering brine.
Wrenching me they fling me shorewards –
These three fierce young men –
Until they lash me to a surfboard
And sail me in facedown the final furlong,
The final rumble strips of foam,

Racing the shoreline, beaching me,
Dumping me on wet sand bereft of ocean,
Raising me up by the armpits, hauling me.
On my hands and knees
In amber froth
I crawl the final metre.
On the keel of an upturned boat I sat down
And wept and shivered and stretched to vomit.
Sat retching there like a shredded parsnip,
The cowering genius of the shore.
Another Bondi casualty bent forlorn
Upon the tourist shingles
Of New South Wales.

When I am able to look up
My three midwives have gone
Whose names I do not know,
Only Brian. The two together
Were English boys. They waddled off
Into the anonymity of selflessness –
"All part of the lifesaver's ethos"
It is explained to me weeks later by
The North Bondi Surf Life-Saving Club.
Drowning and trying to wave
And not being seen
But being heard in the nick of time.
On the instructions of Brian,
With Gerard's help,
I present myself
At the Bondi Medical Centre,
34 Campbell Parade.
A young Chinese doctor who cannot help
In spite of his instinctive etiquette

Smirking at my ludicrous appearance –
Trouserless in a green blazer –
Applies a stethoscope to my spine
And chimes: "Sir, you're fine."
Dr C. Chin.
35 Australian dollars.
Cash payment.

Gerard drives me to St Ignatius's school
Where for half-an-hour
I play the serious fool
To waves of applause.
That night I do not dare to sleep
But keep on the bedside light
Listening to my own breathing,
The possum in the wainscotting.
Instead of being a cold cod
On a slab in Sydney morgue
I am a warm fish in bed –
How can this be?
What sort of justice is this?
The crab of luck?

May I when I get home,
If I get home,
Chatter less cant
Especially when it comes
To life and death
Or to other people's lives;
May I be
Less glib, less cocky;
May I be
Never righteous.

If I conclude
I ever have the right
To call Ayers Rock "Uluru"
May I be
Not smug about it –
Remember I'm only a white man.
May I take to heart
What the Aboriginal people
Of Brisbane, Alice Springs, Canberra,
Said and did not say to me.
May I never romanticise
The lives of Aboriginal people.
May I never write trite
Codswallop about indigenousness;
May I begin to listen.
May I decipher next time
Silences under gum trees:
"Give him Bondi!"

Don't think I will swim
Again in any sea.
Doubt if I will walk
Again by any sea.
But if I do –
If ever again I should have
The cheek to walk
The strand at Keel
In Achill Island –
To walk those three
Skies-in-the-sands miles
By those riding-stable half-doors
Of the Sheik of Inishturk,
With their herds of white horses

Leaning out at me fuming –
I will make that long walk
In nausea as well as awe:
The wings of the butterflies in my stomach
Weighed down by salt for evermore.

Next day I board a Boeing 767
From Sydney to Bangkok
Not caring – glancing over
My shoulder on the tarmac
At Mascot, not caring.
Not caring about anything.
Not about Egypt.
Not about Mayo.
Not about Ireland.
Not even longing for home.
Not even longing for home.
Praying once for all
I am gutted of ego;
That I have at last learnt
The necessity of being nothing,
The XYZ of being nobody.
In so far as I care
May I care nothing for myself,
Care everything for you –
Young mother of two
In the next seat;
A boy and a girl.
Thumbs in their mouths,
Helplessly asleep.
Back in Dublin
One person in whom
I can confide: Colm,

In that brusque,
Anti-sentimental,
Staccato-magnanimous,
Shooting-self-pity-in-the-eye
Tongue of his whispers
On the telephone at noon:
"I swam in Rottnest
Off the coast of Perth,
Nearly lost my . . .
The sea is different in Australia, Paul,
A different pull."

A year later
I cannot sleep
For thinking of Bondi;
Nightly re-enactment
Of being eaten alive
Under bottomless ceilings,
Pillows sprinting above me,
The bedroom window
Declining to open,
A school-yard of faces
Pressing their noses
Against double-glazed glass
Waving at me
Hail or Farewell? –
I cannot know.
I am come into deep waters
Where the floods overflow me.

PART TWO

SONIA AND DONAL
AND TRACEY AND PATRICK

Sonia

I

O my thirty-year-old daughter
On the starting line in Sydney
How I want it to be all over!
Panic hacking
Your attacking face!

What cut of chaos are you being screened
As you stare down into the raw red track?
Can it be worse than when aged six you saw
Between the black floorboards of your yellow bedroom
A spider in the plughole of your father's ear?

The Divine Painter has flung out
Of the skylight His studio brush;
With palette knife He is
Whipping up your forehead!
"It's *my* life," you plead, "*my* life."

O my God, levitating with your knife,
Driving its stiletto into her eyes!
O my thirty-year-old daughter
On the starting line in Sydney
Will I ever greet you the far side of strife?

22 SEPTEMBER 2000

23

Now that you have crossed the finishing line and,
Prancing into the claws of applause,
Jumped up and spun around and smiled that
    wide-eyed smile –
That eyes-in-the-mouth smile –
And packed your bags, flown home across the world,

One day in winter – a Sunday morning
Soaked in suburban snooze –
I will greet you at the park gates and we will go
For a cloistral stroll beneath the emptied trees –
Selfless horse chestnuts drained of sap.

Father, daughter, each in our tracksuits:
The leaking treetops, the puddled grass;
Passing the time of day, not speaking
Until at the Shaky Bridge we kiss goodbye.
I want to make a presentation to you

But without mortifying you. Dearest daughter,
On behalf of all the parents of the Cobh of Cork,
I want to present you with a pewter flask
Of the Waters of Oblivion –
Raw from their source in Gougane Barra.

III

You have earned it, most have not;
We who have evaluated
Your giddiness – your steppe gene.
O Russian cygnet of the Cobh of Cork
If there is a heaven, who would
Petrify to dwell in it? Not you –
Who would rather be a torrent than a gem.
You are, you were, you always will be
A soul in spate, not a precious stone.

25 SEPTEMBER 2000

Donal

to Geraldine Berney

In the heaven-haven
Of Our Lady's Hospice
In your native Harold's Cross
Around your deathbed
Men henpecked like mothers.

Sebastian Barry at the foot
Of your bed explaining
Like an army chaplain's wife
The procedure of dying;
Bob Quinn like a granny
Groaning "I never thought –
I never thought –";
John Cronin like a midwife
Interpreting, adjudicating
Every inhalation, every tremor;
Jimmy Berney at your elbow
Like a sage aunt
Concentrating on prayer;
Brendan Sherry like a seamstress
Fermenting in the wall
With pins between his lips.

Oldfashioned Donal!
Oldfashioned to the end!
How you courted death!
With such grace!

With such ardour!
With such deadpan panache!

Once she gave you her hand
How gallantly you courted her;
Yet on the day of your death –
Death who was your bride
Became your daughter;
All that Saturday in mid-July
Death came chugging up the aisle on
     your arm,
Up the Grand Canal,
Like a barge from Athy
Along the black hairs of your wrist
Past whistling waterhens
And at 10.57 p.m. you gave her away!

In that helter-skelter relay
Of baton change handover
You looked so composed!
Hand over hand.
From your high white pillows
You were gazing down
Into her freckled red face.
How proud you were of her!
You closed your eyes.

Donal macushla,
My dark Donal,
Father of the bride,
The day you died
You gave her away
With such style

That the Chairperson
Of the Crafts Council
Of Ireland
Waved his arm
Above his head
Like Jim Larkin
In O'Connell Street –
Your favourite sculpture –
Because he could find
No words to describe
What he felt
About Donal McCann.
He stammered:
"Such a – such a –
Stylish man!"

Seconds after you died –
Your birthpangs audible
Outside in the corridors –
All of us men-mothers –
All of us hen-men –
Your pals, your cronies –
Ran out into the streets
Onto the airwaves.

For all of the next week
Like pigtailed Hasidim at the Wailing Wall
We proclaimed your birth to the Nation.
On the steps of the Temple
Sat the Nation's Cantors –
David Hanly, Eamon Dunphy –
The stones of their microphones
On chains around their necks –

Solemnly chanting your birth,
"A saviour has been born to us and . . ."

Even the brats of the Nation
Got in on the act,
Myers & Co,
Spoilt brats preaching to us
About the sins of Donal McCann,
Making us grin with their
Larks of pomposity,
Their pranks of hypocrisy,
Although once or twice
As they upstaged one another –
How you detested upstaging! –
Little did they know
How close they were
To earning a clip on the ear
From Master McCann.

O you who taught me,
Dead Donal,
The truth of the art
Of the tragicomedy of Christianity –
The fact of the Resurrection,
The logic of the Crucifixion –
Have mercy on Myers and me.
At the end of the Comedy
Are we all about to be?

Baptism, communion,
Confirmation, marriage,
Ordination, extreme unction –
Not omitting confession! –

All seven sacraments
Going hell–for–leather
Pell–mell up–hill
Like the *peleton*
In the umbrageous sun –
Ten down,
Three across –
You with your hands
On your knees at the TV
Roaring at them.
At all of us,
To keep our heads down,
To keep our eyes
On the words,
Cycling into the sun,
Into the business of no one;
Into the mud on the peak
Of Alpe d'Huez, to die
Or to nearly die
On the side of the road,
Who knows?
God knows.

O Dearest Donal!
Dead Donal!
Piece of my heart!
Immortal clown!
Black and white
In technicolour!
A smile is general
All over Ireland.

Homage to Tracey Emin

I

Apart from being a unique work of art
What appals me about Tracey Emin's bedroom
Is how similar it is to my own bedroom –
Same white sheets the colour of stagnant dishwater –
Same worndown, wornout, scruffy slippers,
Punched out pill sachets, underwear, price tags –
U–W Bra White 32C £31.00 –
One unopened bottle of *Orangina*
And in blue neon in the ceiling
The legend as in my own bedroom
Every Part Of Me's Bleeding
And I drink much of the night
And I stay in bed in the morning.

Tracey Emin is a seaside of fresh air.
Tracey Emin is the T. S. Eliot *de nos jours*.
Tracey Emin on Margate Sands
    can connect nothing with nothing.
Inside every fluid human
A small girl is frozen
In the wings waiting to walk on
To ask the sixty-thousand dollar question
At the Cardinal's Ball:
Where does the holy water come from?

II

That autumn the winds came and blew the leaves off
    the trees
And there were leaves stuck to the windscreens of the cars
And I saw that the lines on my face were pleasant places
And I took the first flight out of Gatwick
To go find my father on the shores of Cyprus.

Father, will you swim with me in the high seas?
Will we jump together?

Tracey, Tracey, hold on tight

7 DECEMBER 1999

The Death of the Legendary Dr Patrick Nugent, G.P., 6 October 1999

to Sybille

In that point nought nought one
Of a fraction of a second
In the sunflower hospice
When you flew over the bar
Performing your fantastic
"Nugent Flop",
A woman in red and blue
Stepped forward to greet you.
She inquired: "Dr Nugent?
The legendary Dr Nugent?"
You blushed and she smiled again,
And then she was gone.
You were left alone in the dark.
You asked: "Where am I?"
You slid down into an aisle seat.
A screen. Credits roll.
"Is this a cinema? Or an aeroplane?
A flying cinema? Air France?"
Sybille inside you,
John McGahern behind you.
"The writer! Charming chap!"
You settled into your seat,
Fastened your seat-belt,
Glad to be there, safe in the dark,

Chuffed that the usherette had said:
"The legendary Dr Nugent."
Although you preferred
The company of women,
You had not expected
God to be a woman.
Losing the head, Brother Neckerman
Had protested that God is a man!
In spite of your star-struck faith
It had not dawned on you
In all of your fifty-eight years
That God is a cinema usherette.
Winking, you lit a cigarette:
Everything rhymes –
Just like old times!

Reading McGahern

Abandon me to despair's surprise:
To the open endings of my days.

Portrait of the Artist

At closing time on Saturday nights in winter,
Off Grafton Street in Dublin in the 1950s,
He was a young creamy bull stamping his hooves
On pavements, goring, butting, bellowing, bleeding,
Straining at the neck and being restrained
By stringy maidens in waist-length plaits.

Monday mornings he'd appear in the District Court,
Eyes closed, lips swollen violet to the cheekbone.
Thursdays he'd draw a beauty with charcoal
And with crayon he had the nerve of Degas.
We watched and waited
While he chose New York or Paris or Rome.

He stayed at home and he never joined
Any coterie – coy or callous;
Never licked the buttock of any clique.
He was so political he was anti-political.
Wild red deer. Extinction!
He became a creature of the Forest of Nothing.

This August morning – the first morning of autumn –
Warm, moist, smoky, leaf-splattered –
Rowing his stick across Baggot Street Bridge –
A simulacrum of Pollock in old age:
Lean the meat of the old bull of Wyoming;
Debonair, puckish, streetwise countryman.

Limp roll-up stuck to his upper lip;
Sporting a spotless cream linen jacket,
A canary yellow shirt open at the neck,
Olive-green pressed trousers and a pair
Of polished, spit-in-your-eye, tan, laced brogues.
Disinterested in clichés of recognition.

Blarneyless, he invites me
To have "a jar" with him in the Waterloo House,
Whose proprietor Andy Ryan – he imparts to me –
Has sold the House for two million.
"I see him in the street smiling like a hen –
An ould hen sitting on two million!"

Over glasses – Heineken for him, Ginger Ale for me –
In response to a query from myself, he smiles
That there was none handier in our time than Paul Klee.
He is quiet with glee about the light in Mayo –
But also, he mutters, the quality of its dark.
He drawls: "I miss listening to the dark in Mayo."

Artist knowing what he wants and does not want
He is as nonchalant as he was
Fifty-five easel-courting years ago;
He whom now no trend-editor can identify.
Leaning on his stick he growls "Goodbye"
And steps away to work another year alone.

7 AUGUST 1999

37

Charles Brady's Irish Painter

Camouflaged under a willow tree in Rossnaree,
    Solo in a coracle conceived for three,
Blinking up out from under her black beret,
    Camille Souter – war refugee.

The Bunnacurry Scurry

O Deirdre, meet Deirdre
   Of the sleet-on-the-mountainpeaks smile,
   Sumps-of-streams eyes,
   Bog cotton in your hair
   With your Harry,
Like you I'm in a hurry –
   In a delicate hurry –
To do the Bunnacurry Scurry.

Once, before time began,
   When we were in our teens,
It was the Dooagh Rock,
   The Innishbiggle Skiffle,
   The Dookinella March,
   The Crumpaun Jig,
   The Dooniver Hornpipe,
   The Saula Hucklebuck,
   The Valley Waltz,
But now in May ninety-nine,
   In the primes of our lives,
It is the Bunnacurry Scurry.

I meet Phil in the Caravanserai –
   Phil McHugh that's married to Peadar –
Peadar the TV repair man who loves TV sets so
   much, says Vi (approaching ninety but doing
   fifty-five), that he holds on to sets for days and
    weeks
   and months and years and eras and centuries –

I'm on my way back from Teddy Lavelle's –
Teddy that's married to Margaret –
From not getting the one *Independent on Sunday*
        that did not come in
When everything else came in including the *Observer*
        and *The News of the World*
Just as yesterday the one *Guardian on Saturday*
        did not come in.
Phil gives me the last *Sunday Times* on Achill Island,
        with its Hieronymus Bosch cover of the
            postmodern, glittering
        snake's belly of hackette Terry Keane
            masticating wads of sterling
        notes whilst vomiting up her lover's guts.
Quare stuff to be gawking at after ten o'clock Mass.

Once, before time began,
        When we were in our teens,
It was the Dooagh Rock,
        The Innishbiggle Skiffle,
        The Dookinella March,
        The Crumpaun Jig,
        The Dooniver Hornpipe,
        The Saula Hucklebuck,
        The Valley Waltz,
        The Cabin Fever,
But now in May ninety-nine,
        In the primes of our lives,
It is the Bunnacurry Scurry.

When I come to Achill on holiday or sabbatical
It is not of course for a holiday or sabbatical.

I come to do a year's work in a week.
I come to dress in green and blue,
Browns, yellows, greys.
I come to do the Bunnacurry Scurry.
Midmornings I do not go down –
Much as I crave conversations of affection –
To Mary Hoban's garden on the mountain,
Or to Mikey O'Malley's post office at Keel
Or to Maeve Calvey's diner for breakfast
Or to Alice's P.O. in Dugort
Or to P.J.'s Seal Caves on the strand,
Stopping in the ditch with delight to let
Ann Fuchs in her yellow Volks wheel past;
Instead I scurry around the bog to the back
        of the mountain and back –
The Bunnacurry Scurry.

Once, before time began,
        When we were in our teens,
It was the Dooagh Rock,
        The Innishbiggle Skiffle,
        The Dookinella March,
        The Crumpaun Jig,
        The Dooniver Hornpipe,
        The Saula Hucklebuck,
        The Valley Waltz,
        The Cabin Fever,
        The Sound Jive,
But now in May ninety-nine,
        In the primes of our lives,
It is the Bunnacurry Scurry.

Is the mist down for the day?
Will it lift in an hour?
Have you noticed in the last twenty minutes
A brightening in the sky –
A slight, slight brightening
Of the sky over Blacksod?
Will you go Newport or Ballycroy
On the road home to Toome?

Once, before time began,
        When we were in our teens,
It was the Dooagh Rock,
        The Innishbiggle Skiffle,
        The Dookinella March,
        The Crumpaun Jig,
        The Dooniver Hornpipe,
        The Saula Hucklebuck,
        The Valley Waltz,
        The Cabin Fever,
        The Sound Jive,
        The Dugort Foxtrot,
But now in May ninety-nine,
        In the primes of our lives,
It is the Bunnacurry Scurry.

23 MAY 1999

No. 13, Est. 1928
McKennas Barber

to Síabhra MacBride Walsh

I step in out of the pelting rain;
The barber murmurs "A damp day".
I cite the east wind. He inclines fractionally –
"With the east wind, sir, the rain is usually dry."

"Lean your head forward into the basin, sir."
Threading his fingers through my sudded hair,
The guitar of my scalp forks him up chords
Which he plucks with suckling care.

His fingertips are so maternal-feminine
I cannot help but be his cosseted lover;
He makes the young girls in the Unisex Salon
Seem elder savages at their callous combing.

In the off-white vase of my skull
The barber arranges the orchids of my soul;
Snipping stems, lopping stalks,
Sacrificing the part for the sake of the whole.

Oh what have I done but open a
Foam glass shop door in the County of Mayo
On Monday the 20th of September 99
And stepped into a cellar in Austria?

In 1790, low-ceilinged, in a drawer
I detect pocked parchment by Mozart,
Not identified by human eyes before,
But stalked over by a reticent spider.

From left to right across the page
Scissors scurry, dart, divide, partner;
Hairs like silences swoon down onto the lino;
The barber invites me to look into the mirror.

I behold my slowly ticking face
Beaming out from under a haycock of cadenza;
Fiddlers and whistlers all pausing together;
"That'll be £6.80, sir, and thank you."

Auntie Gerry's Favourite Married Nephew Seamus

After dropping his eldest boy back to boarding school
Seamus was driving home to Athlone with another man
When he came upon a woman hitching a lift.
He lifted her and the next thing –
She offered him sex. In the car!
Seamus was shell-shocked.
It's a miracle he didn't crash.
He was very embarrassed!
In front of the other man!
But as I said to him on the phone –
In a crisis he always phones me –
Wasn't he lucky that he wasn't alone?
That he had the other man with him?

Spokes Embracing on the Banks of the Brisbane

O my green fool
Do not sketch us as lechers
Or as a pair of dogs copulating.

We are a couple
Of wheelchair lovers making
Brisbane under a weeping fig.

Head Hunters

I got my hair cut in Alice Springs
In *Head Hunters* on the Todd River.

White man: *Aboriginals have a lot in common with the
    Irish.*
Aboriginal: *Yes – we even look like the Irish.*

Garbo

It's the thing to be:
To be no one.

Scavenging in pain
For the grave of Garbo
In the Pine Cemetery
In Skogskyrkogarden
In the southern suburbs
Of Stockholm
Three hours in the sun,
Quick to give up the ghost.

I believe in the Eucharist
Of the nothingness of life.

Time to tap out a flit
From the cemetery maze;
Take the T-ban
Back into Gamla Stan;
Traipse down Kopsmangatan;
Gable-gaze
Over a bowl of latte;
Be left alone.

I believe in the Eucharist
Of the nothingness of life.

Popping painkillers –
High rises of my vertebrae
Lit up with pain
(I have no
Medical Insurance),
I cling to the wall
Of the Mortuary Chapel;
An intestinal fellow in blue
Slips out and I blurt:
"Where is Garbo?"

I believe in the Eucharist
Of the nothingness of life.

He nods: "I show you."
He turns on his heel,
Lopes back into the garden
Of the Mortuary Chapel.
He asks: "Where you from?"
"Ireland."
He half-laughs:
"I fly Ryanair – once."

I believe in the Eucharist
Of the nothingness of life.

He steps out the far wall
Of the Mortuary Garden;
Down, up, flights of steps,
Terraces of headstones.
We arrive at an earthen,
Grass-topped ringfort,

Raised up, bare,
Twenty metres wide,
Fringed by twelve
Young weeping willows.

I believe in the Eucharist
Of the nothingness of life.

Upstage in the glade
One small solitary headstone
Of coral-pink marble;
No date, no conventional phrase;
No eighteenth-century bombast;
No sententious solipsism.
An autograph stencilled in marble:
      Greta Garbo.

I believe in the Eucharist
Of the nothingness of life.

Sleep, girl, sleep.
But you do not sleep;
Bluey, yellowy corpse,
Daydreaming;
Floating on the wind;
Scot-free,
Above the tops
Of the Scots pine.

I believe in the Eucharist
Of the nothingness of life.

To be a boy or a girl –
An emancipated slave –
A freed adolescent –
Recline on your spine
In the ashes of your bones.
Glance up at the blue,
Gold above the pines.
At the grave of Garbo
Waiting to die.
Extinguish me.

It's the thing to be:
To be no one.

30 AUGUST 1999

The Great Cathedral of Stockholm

A man slumped over a pew:
Between the shoulderblades being massaged by *You*.

Under the Bank of Sweden

Under the Bank of Sweden
I recite my poems
With my hands by my sides.

Passers-by stop, start.
Stare, look away.
Mums shunt buggies.

Under the arch of the Bank,
Young Sergei of Voronezh
Is bursting adagios on a silver trumpet.

I recite from my soles.
My head tilts back.
My eyes wring shut.

I hear a five-crown coin
Clink in my plate.
I am a free man.

That Swedish wife
Might not after all
Be a chimera!

She might be that experimental
Physiotherapist next pitch –
A pioneer of salutagenesis.

We might construct a shack on a skerry.
I might take root in the Scandinavian sun
Of her soul, she in mine.

She will work all over.
In the nights I will read to her
For as long as she wants me to:

Gunnar Myrdal;
Dag Hammarskjöld;
Göran Sonnevi.

She will swim asleep in the fourth
Paragraph and I will swim asleep
To the *more, more* of her placid snore.

Two young silver-haired bankers
Like baboons clamber into a black limo
Without glaring me a glance.

Ah glare me a glance.
Ah do. Ah do.
Ah glare me an old Uppsala glance.

A small, blonde, sturdy woman
Skims a ten-crown note into my plate,
Blushing peach cheeks as she curtseys.

Young Sergei of Voronezh
Does not know it, but under the Bank of Sweden
He is accompanying me on my Milky Way to Estonia.

The night ferry to Tallinn:
The rendezvous with my great-grandmother;
The beginning of my new death.

O Patrick, I am happier
Than I have ever been
Under the Bank of Sweden.

The 24,000 Islands of Stockholm

How you do pontificate
About the politics
Of Stockholm –
About how too sedate,
Too predictable
Are the politics of Stockholm;
How the politics of Stockholm
Are like the citizens of Stockholm,
Too rational, too clinical.

On, on, you sermonise
About the Swedish Academy;
How the waters are awash
With bobbing condoms.
I doubt – but keep
The thought to myself –
That condoms "bob",
Whatever their content
Or lack of content.

Have you nothing to say
About the islands –
The 24,000 islands of Stockholm?
Nothing?
About even, say, a single skerry?
A rock, a pine, a hut?
Nothing?
Not even about one of them?
One of the 24,000
Islands of Stockholm?

Nothing about skimming
With forefinger and thumb
Water-rolled slivers
Of infant granite?
Nothing about how oaks
Can conceive in crevices
On a rock in the Baltic?
Nothing about why
A man and a woman
Might choose to be sparse
On an island in Stockholm?
Nothing about how the Bergman
Question posed by the Garden
Of Eden is whether a human
Can handle leisure or not?
About the origin of deprivation?
About whether or not
The Goth has got it right
In the islands of Stockholm –
In the 24,000
Islands of Stockholm?

29 AUGUST 1999

On Giving a Poetry Recital to an Empty Hall

to Theo Dorgan

The engagement was to recite for one hour
At the Ballyfree Community Arts Festival,
And I did, and I gave it my all
To the empty hall.

The empty chairs gazed up at me in awe.
I caught the eye of a chair in the third row
And it would not let go,
Toying with my plight.
A redheaded, dumpy chair on the edge that never
        once smiled,
And the more droll my poem, the more it pouted.

When I had done, the Chairman of the Committee
Before even the non-applause had died down
Scrambled up onto the podium.
He spoke with brusque authority
And at length
About the significance of poetry in the new
        millennium
And how it is always so much more congenial
To have a small audience or, better still,
No audience at all.
"It's more intimate," he sighed piously, "it's more
        intimate."
And he blew his nose and he shrieked:

Go raibh míle maith agaibh go léir –
To you all a thousand thank you's!
He turned to me and he winked and he muttered:
"That's the last poetry recital we'll have in this town."

Murphy's Farewell

I

– Oh Mike, don't be mad at me!

– Paul, I am about to don my shades and go back down through economy class to the driving range in the tail of the plane – in the *tail* of the plane – and under no circumstances do I want to be intruded upon, and if the *Fasten Your Seat Belt* sign comes on I'll fasten my own *portable* seat belt and keep on driving and driving – my Christy O'Connor swing, once unfurled, it just keeps on swinging and swinging and swinging – no matter what the turbulence I'll keep on driving and driving, finding my range and finding my range and all the time thinking of dear old middle-aged Cardinal O Fiaich of beloved memory on the 3 p.m. *Aer Lingus* flight back from Rome on 10 October 1982 in thunder and lightning over the Pyrenees and he *strap-hanging* in the aisle with a cigarette *Carrolls No 1* making yellow manure of the fingers of his right hand – his *right* hand! – and he chatting about ecumenism and architecture to Peter Pearson who is a Quaker – Peter Pearson is a *great* Quaker – and all the life-loving *Aer Lingus* hostesses too in awe of His Eminence to say, "Your Eminence, it is considered not right and fitting to strap-hang at 36,000 feet in an electrical storm with a lighted cigarette in your hand," because, you see, Paul, when all is shrugged off or not shrugged off, it's a long way to Orlando, Florida, it's a long long way to Orlando, Florida, it's an awful long long way to Orlando, Florida, and never did I cast the first stone nor indeed never did affable, courteous, convivial Cardinal O'Fiaich – had I not become a broadcaster I would quite likely have been a Cardinal. Cardinal Murphy of Orlando, Florida, bugger the begrudgers.

II

The Laughter Existentialist – that was he.
A serious man for the laughter.
If you canoe'd far enough into the crocodile glades of
 his glee
You came upon a silent, neglected jetty.

From Kierkegaard to the Marx Brothers and Chaplin
Via Jack Cruise and Laurel and Hardy;
From Maureen Potter to Albert Camus –
Is it possible to laugh on the neglected jetty

Of the world? Is it possible to be polite
In an evil place? To be courteous
In an evil time? To be politely drastic
And simultaneously enthusiastic?

In his Mike-in-the-Box way he was a dead serious
 man
Up to his neck in the sands of Carnival!
Who will know about all that sunken gold of affection
Until long after the Friday night of Murphy's
 Farewell?

Until long after the Friday night of Murphy's Farewell.

19 MAY 2000

The Death of the Mother
of the Dalai Lama

to Dr Patrick Nugent

Sitting up in bed, waiting to die –
Root-and-branch pain –
Brooklyn Bridge
Seems to me to be swaying
Inside its plain black frame.

My son, my dutiful son,
Brought it back from New York
After he visited the United Nations.
Hung it himself on the wall
At the foot of my bed.

My son, my thoughtful son,
He remembered to come
Armed with hammer and nail
In his shoulder bag,
Asked me which wall.

At the foot of the bed, I said.
After he'd gone I asked
My sister to take down
Everything else in the room.
Leave me alone with Brooklyn Bridge –

Brooklyn Bridge which
Seems to me to be swaying
Inside its black frame.
Bumble bee in Milky Way.
My son, my dutiful, my thoughtful, my
    good-as-gold son.

Night-Elegy for Thérèse Cronin

The living pray to the living to recognise difference

Thérèse, black though the day be –
Blackest of January –
Grand Canal in flood –
Darkness at noon –
Raining cats and dogs
On ducks and drakes –
Drenched reeds and supermarket trolleys
Emerge thriving on your glamorous beauty.

At Huband Bridge under a silver birch,
My collar turned up, my cap pulled down,
Like Tony on the road to Moscow,
Feeling like I think you must feel
In your death – coming into your own
Into the heart of the heartless world.

Under the redbrick wall
Not of the Kremlin
But of *Sun Microsystems Ireland*,
One lone black waterhen
With green legs – green legs, Thérèse! –
And red-and-yellow beak!

Past Baggot Street Bridge
Swirling out of the West
I pass P.K. on his seat
Stopping out in the rain,

Bareheaded, with the hat beside him
For company, a pair of swans
Crossing the bar of his gaze.

Calm cob, calm pen
Not for the first time nor for the last,
Stopping out in the rain, Thérèse,
Stopping out in the rain.

7 JANUARY 1999

In Memoriam Sister Mary Magdalena, Martyr (1910–99)

I was born in Westport, County Mayo,
At the start of the blackest century;
Christened Una, third daughter
Of Joseph and Eileen MacBride.
I saw my father taken hostage
By the Black and Tans,
Sunbathed on the rocks of Murrisk,
Played tennis with bank clerks
In the 1920's, spoke French,
Bicycled free in France,
Became a nun of the Holy Faith,
From the North Wall
Sailed for Trinidad in the 1940s
To become a schoolteacher in Couva.

Only thirty-seven years of age
I made my home in Trinidad,
Loved the people as they loved me.
In Trinidad I could be myself;
Could be the girl I always was,
The soul of the party, the Irish nun
Who could not stop laughing;
Could be a friend to Thee
In spite of a jealous bourgeoisie;
Permitted to revisit Ireland
Every five or six years
To see my mother for a day.

Forty years bicycled by
Until too wiped out
To support myself in Trinidad
I was brought back to the mother house
In Dublin in Glasnevin
On Tolka's northern banks.
There, as I knew I would be,
I was arrested by Alzheimer,
But not before I took the gospel chance –
My scriptural prerogative –
To speak from the dock
To the community in the convent chapel:

"I want you to hang me up in the chapel tonight
Head down by the ankles crossed
Christ O Jesus
And cut me open and drain off my blood
And brim up all the chaste enamel buckets
And tiptoe out onto the banks of Tolka
And empty the buckets out into the stars –
Out into the black river of stars –
The believable stars of the night sky.
I want you to stand on Glasnevin hill,
Dearest Sisters of the Holy Faith,
While my blood floods off into the stars –
The Bloody Way:
In which I see
My life and death rhyme
Across the night of time."

New Year's Eve, 1999

Thank Ophelia that's all over –
Eileen Dubh, Greta Garbo –
One thousand years of teens!
But will our twenties
Be any wonderfuller?
Up the cul-de-sac behind every disco,
Creeps & fiends?

O tomorrow let's be warm
Who today are cool.

It's 3001 I pine for:
The treeline of fiction;
Children of the New Forest;
Our Lady of the Fertile Rock;
You and I –
A pilot and a doctor
Of the fertile ice.

O tomorrow let's be warm
Who today are cool.

What a cheesy scene
Adolescence has been!
The Black Plague when I was thirteen,
Wars of Religion at sixteen,
Famine at eighteen,
AIDS when I was nineteen,
Cromwell, Hitler in between.

68

O tomorrow let's be warm
Who today are cool.

Countdown to 11.27,
Nuzzle noses at 11.38,
Fire off our retro-rockets at 11.49,
Up into our goosepimples at 11.53,
Zapping in the Eye of Midnight
A space shuttle docking – spraying soft slow sticky
        stuff o'er all the beanbags and the screens!
Another small-screen step for kinderkind!

O tomorrow let's be warm
Who today are cool.

In Memoriam Liam Walsh

for Pam

A week ago this morning I was a man hard at work:
This morning I am a sparrow of smoke over Croagh Patrick.

26 OCTOBER 2000

The Neighbour

Isn't it terrible about the Kursk?
In 1981 I picked up a copy –
I don't read much –
Of Chekhov's plays and –
I'm not –
Wait till I tell you –
The Cherry Orchard –
Now I read it every winter.

21 AUGUST 2000

PART THREE

EARLY CHRISTIAN
IRELAND WEDDING CRY

Early Christian Ireland Wedding Cry

And now that these two earthlings have been by the
    poet-priest blessed
I will be able to telephone Sarah and burst out
"May I speak to your *husband*?"
Or to telephone Mark and burst out
"May I speak to your *wife*?"
How knees-on-the-full-moon I will feel to bawl
Such interstellar language: "Husband", "wife" –
Vocabulary as prehistoric as a tree.
Children – to see the world – climb the treetops of
    matrimony.
It was for matrimony that we earthlings espoused language;
"Husband", "wife". Eureka!
The waters of reality are spousal – Gerard Manley
    Archimedes.
Be it manmade canal or iceage mountain stream,
Water is hand-over-hand, pooled magnanimity.

II

Mark Joyce, Sarah Durcan, we thank you
For shepherding us all to this far, secret, idyllic niche;
Nephin, Lough Conn, Rake Street, Enniscoe.

By marrying each other, you are marrying us
To the marriage place – to the mountain
And to the lake; to the street and to the house.

Long after this afternoon is mustard ashes,
Our eyes will remain upon the mountain,
Sipping insights from our primary sources:

All our childhoods – all those eras:
All those epochs of contemplation when it was nothing
To spend all day on the lakeshore gazing upon the waters;

The unfathomable ticking of one's own heart;
The inscrutable parades of waves;
The unimaginable bottom of the lake.

All those rain curtains of Sunday afternoons
Driving up to Enniscoe House to see what it looked like
And to glean what could be gleaned from the prospect.

All those six-month summers gazing upon the mountain,
Robed in her grey blueness over Conn;
Taliswoman of our fortune and our fate;

Deferring to her for our stimulation and our aim.
Waiting for her to wash herself in a dawn sky
Her man assembles their abode of grass and rain.

III

Marriage is the sunrise of contemplation
In which two creatures compose themselves
Inside the catastrophe of war.
Each is the other's cloak and asylum.
In the last of the light they cleave to one another
On the barbed-wire shore.

Back to back in the weeping and warring night
One sleeps while the other tracks
The cracks upon the moon-stacked windowpane;
The other sleeps and the one awakes
To track a snail shadowing the moon
On that polar hike across the cracked glass.
You are the meaning of my life
And I of yours – the piscina in the niche.

IV

On Midsummer's Day when this chapel was being built,
A housepainter from Lahardaun cried from his ladder:
"Raise high the roofbeams, carpenter!
On Midsummer's Day a hundred years from now
A Durcan will step into this chapel to marry a Joyce!
The tabernacle will needs be inserted in the wall!
Needs be rakes of candlestick racks!
These Joyces and these Durcans – in their communions,
They are fierce people for the lighting of candles!
Needs be also the outside freshly whitewashed
For these two will also be painters!
Members of the craft as well as of the wedding!
We will need burial grounds around the chapel
Because these two will also be philosophers
Who ponder mortality –
How mortality is the mother of integrity."

V

All things come in twos – which is why
Marriage is the paradigm of science.
The code of all physics and all chemistry is marriage;
The figure of all energy is two.
Caspar the Cat, I dive round the villages of Mayo –
Hollymount, Roundfort, Turlough, Straide –
Doff my Castlebar hat with its white cockade,
Lean upon my Westport stick with its brass ferrule,
And twinkling at the gate of the scythed hayfield
At the top of Rake Street
I wait for thee, my love, to take my arm
And be my spouse for now and evermore.
One by one we enter the aisle of Rake Street
In order to exit it as two.

VI

By the waters of Conn, under the eye of Nephin,
We sit down and kneel and laugh and pray.
Cloud systems that began their lives in Labrador
Empty their waters on Nephin's peaks;
Mountain streams charge down the mountainside
Past the two-light east window, the lake
Brims, turns over on its sleeping side,
Yawns, smiles, frowns, goes on
Dreaming its 600 million-year-old dream –
This is where the Durcans and the Joyces hail from:
Our dreamspace, the County of Mayo!
We – the wedding guests – die out of the frame
Leaving Mark and Sarah alone in the storm,

Secure in the fleece of the sheep of the yew tree,
Their foreheads thumbed by the asylum-seeker Christ
Who stowed away into earthlingland to secrete compassion;
Leaving them in peace – together, each to each –
Let us now praise these waters and the mountain:
The sleeping woman with her waking man.

21 JUNE 2000

PART FOUR

CRIES OF AN IRISH CAVEMAN

Cries of an Irish Caveman

I

Every day on the off-chance –
On the ten million-to-one chance –
You might knock on my door
I organise my cave and make my bed.

II

In my bed alone at night I press
My face down deep
Into the cold, white, Egyptian
Cotton pillow of your soul.

III

My arms are empty all for the want of thee:
A pair of arms on the rampage in a crypt.

IV

With whom do you shower?
Do you complete the circle?

V

You who dared me love define:
Love is to see the story in a line.

VI

I drive past your villa on a whim:
Hoping you are out, hoping you are in.

VII

An interloper forceps your name up out of chat:
I stifle a bawl.

VIII

But most of all I miss your laugh:
Your haughtiness's hot bath.

IX

What am I doing standing on no legs outside your
    gate?
Gargling, only gargling.

X

When in a restaurant behind Victoria railway station
Your name is spoken, my stomach lets drop its plates.

XI

Last night in Hammersmith the barman saw you with
    Greg.
So that's who it is! Greg!

XII

I am sitting alone in my cave on Friday afternoon.
You have gone to bed for the weekend with your
    new man.

XIII

I am rocking in the bay of your rejection.
Becalmed in the nirvana of my defeat.

XIV

Beethoven fell out of his podium in love with Teresa.
Arrarra.

XV

All the hot day long your bladderwrack detonates salt
    water.
All the cold night long my berries bleed.

XVI

I think of you and he lounging in The Rose and Goat:
The suction of your lipstick, he clearing his throat.

XVII

On my answer machine I hear you say "See you in the
    next century".
I stoop into the wrecking ball of the future.

XVIII

I fly over to London and search Hammersmith for you.
Not a trace of you in the hot sardine guts of the pubs.

XIX

You know I know you know the choreography of my
    humiliation:
My flesh spancelled, my soul bellowing.

XX

A practical woman like you cannot bear to hear
That ejaculation of terror – "I love you".

XXI

What is it? Above all, your voice!
Your voice with its gloved hands!

XXII

I see his head upon your pillow.
I snatch at my nail scissors.

XXIII

I believe that you will come back to me
Although I know you will not.

XXIV

After your social phonecall, I brushed my hair with
    toothpaste.
And there was peace on the sofa.

XXV

I stare across the flooded river at your villa:
I am a Russian at the Finish of Love.

XXVI

Ethics are the co-ordinates of aesthetics:
How to live with the living, how to die with the dead.

XXVII

There is no more peaceful way to spend
    a brutal winter in the north
Than every afternoon at the cavedoor alone
    drawing you, colouring you in.

XXVIII

Driving through Oola I glare at the derelict petrol pump;
Why are you not standing there filling up your tank?

XXIX

In the hotels of the world I ask always for a double bed:
To turn over on my side and caress your abstract head.

XXX

That a man does not bleed does not mean a man cheats:
A man also has problems with sheets.

XXXI

The scene of the accident is awfuller than the actual
    accident:
Incinerated intimacy, charred seats.

XXXII

Two months since you left a message on my answer
    machine:
I play it back every day – Cita's Theme!

XXXIII

The odd time it rings I clutch at the phone:
It's not you, and I cut myself down.

XXXIV

In sleet I slink out to the supermarket.
Checkout girls; heads down; no eye contact.

XXXV

From pub to pub in Hammersmith:
Tossing the poleaxe after the chainsaw.

XXXVI

Muttering to my bookspines on the shelves of my cave:
Will they also one day walk out on me?

XXXVII

Drawing on my walls keeps me sane:
With my fingers, smudges of green.

XXXVIII

I have two TVs in my cave
But I only watch them four hours a day.
I crouch – an amputee –
And tweezer my eyebrows or the walls.
I am scratching the surface:
A cow, a woman, a bucket.

XXXIX

If my end is to be whooping it up in the Alzheimer's
    disco
It'll be for you I'll be whooping – the lady that's known
    as Cita.

The Origin of Species

Christ on my cave wall
Is as indecipherable as Christ was
        When I used to exist in the future;
Christ waits with God-forsaken patience
        For my sub-Saharan fingertips to trace his face.

Existing in prehistoric time
Is as unimaginable and unthinkable
        As existing in 2001:
Yet here I am in my cave
        Interpreting the silence as far as I can.

It is 8001 BC and Christ –
Derided by the scribes of the tribe,
        Dubbed unclean, locked in the asylum
And the key thrown away – and I
        In the next cave a silence share with him;

Bread of silence break
Into insights in the starry dark;
        He defies me to draw my words
And so it is that in the starry dark
        I draw my words on my cave walls.

The wind cannot blow out my words
Nor the tribunal lawyers, nor the opinion journalists;
        They can snuff out my candles
But not my words drawn on my cave walls.
        Christ, all-fathering mother!

Bovinity

It's not something you're born with,
Like a mouth or an eye.
It's something you detect and cultivate –
It's something you divine –
Bovinity!
Ignoring the crack of her whip,
Flicking my tail.

I am a middle of the road cow.

I like to sit down in the middle of the road,
Curl up and up, before and behind,
Wind my tail around and around myself,
And, accumulating all my flesh and all my soul,
Watch the world go by:
Watch the traffic slowing down and circling round me
Or turn my head away to browse in the horizon.
I have only one preoccupation in existence and that
    is affection.
In the middle of the road all day
On affection I ruminate.

Cowlady – who stole my love away
In the twilight of time –
Blow your horn or flash your lights
But I am staying in the middle of the road
Where I belong. You go and join
The club of logic, on the left or right.

Bovinity!
Raising one hoof, tendering it
Out over the precipice of the cliff,
Drawing the air, all
500 feet of air
Above the sea below,
Withdrawing it.
Bovinity!

It's not something you're born with,
Like a mouth or an eye.
It's something you detect and cultivate –
It's something you divine –
Bovinity!
Ignoring the crack of her whip,
Flicking my tail.

Love at First Sight

Snoozing facedown in the waters of her queensize
    double bed
At 7 a.m. in the cold black dark of a December morning,
It dawned on her that the mellow bellowing under her sash
    window
Was not the massed choirs of the "Ode to Joy"
But a stray cow amok in her flowerbeds. She somersaulted –
All forty-odd years of her –
All five feet two inches of her –
Out of her bed in samurai-style and flung
Herself down the spiral staircase, not hesitating even
To fling an old woolly cardigan over her shoulders,
Unbolted the hall door and skidded out down the stone
    steps
In her white cotton nightgown to confront the loose cow
    astray in her bulbs.

She snatched me by the ear – "So, no tag on your ear?"
She whispered, and she led me by the ear back up the stone
    steps,
Into the coral-pink hall with its ancestral portrait and its
    chandelier,
Up the spiral staircase past the stained-glass window.
She chuckled: "Do I smell whiskey in your fumes?"
On up into her white bedroom with the mahogany chest of
    drawers,
The mahogany dressing table, the mahogany wardrobe with
    mirrors,

On up into her queensize double bed where we spent
All of the next fourteen days –
All 326 hours of them – climbing up out of its plains and
     mountains
Only to perform routine evacuations.

She chirped: The happiest fourteen days of my life.
I boomed harmoniously: Me too.
She laughed: So, you've no tag on your ear?
I quaked: It's no laughing matter.
She said: Are you certain you have no tag?
I blushed: I am certain I have no tag.
She said: No yellow tag?
I said: No yellow tag.
She said: Have you a Department of Agriculture blue
     ID card?
I said: I have no Department of Agriculture blue ID card.
She said: Tell you what I'll do.
I said: What'll you do?
She said: I'll TB and brucellosis test you with my own herd
     and that way you'll be tagged and ID'd.
I said: That's too romantic and kind and conscientious of
     you altogether.
She said: It's the least I can do after what you've given me
     these last fourteen days and, besides, don't I want to
     keep you?
I said: Do you – do you really and truly want to keep me?
She said: Tulip – may I call you Tulip? – I want to keep
     you forever and ever and ever, Tulip – my very own
     tagged and ID'd Tulip.
I mooed: Well, Tulip – I never! You want to keep me
     forever and ever and ever? I never! Do you really?
     And truly?

Toomyvara

When I jerk up my head to watch you jive
Across the hoof-scooped fields to where I'm penned
In the brick paddock by the bicycle-walled stream
It is my ears that babylike weigh me down;
When I see close-up your own pink lobes
Hatched in hair-strands and pierced
By white quartz and know how you can squash
The subtlest tremor in my inner life,
I am a bull bowing to a masked groin:
All I can do is to bellow and to bellow
And to bellow the same name over and over:
Christ Cita! Cita Christ! Cita! Cita!
I rake my hooves and gouge out my clay CV;
I scour my eyes and lick your china body.

The Happy Throng

When in the happy throng I eye your rouged,
Husked head, hair-up, gossiping
And chortling in brass tongues in a wigwam
Of admirers, friends, colleagues, family,
My arms stop by my sides
And I subside into the four-legged beast
That I am and always have been:
A cow upon a furzy headland in the Galtees
Up to my hindquarters in rushes, my eyelids drooping
And my eyes – my fringed, albino eyes –
Corked to capacity with bestial grief;
Staring at you dumbfounded;
I, dribbling, excreting under the dry rain,
Am sealed in detachment, tagged for blame.

The Black Cow of the Family

I am the black cow of the family,
*   Although*
I've a bit of white in me too.

My four sodden legs dumb with cramp
As I sway away from the cliff edge
Peering down at *mein Vater* and *meine Mutter*:
Their drowned corpses glittering
Three hundred feet below;
Trampolining on their spikey spines
And they wail and they sob and they spit and they scold
And they are shrieking out to me:
Join us, join us!
While tight up close behind me
Mein Bruder and *meine Schwester*
As if they are in their billions –
Tutsis and Hutus –
Cavorting in dissonance:
We marry you with machete
In sturm und drang *of confetti.*

I am the black cow of the family,
*   Although*
I've a bit of white in me too.

High-altared alone up here on the cliff,
Leaking blood by the chaliceful,
I rove off to calve
In the next diocese

Where by *mein Gott*
They'll not trace me,
But I am lowing as I lope –
Lowly lowing lamentation –
Off through the veils
Of the rainshowers of my own blood,
Shedding sunlight behind me.

I am the black cow of the family,
            Although
I've a bit of white in me too.

Aaron's Rod

How many forests of hours over nine years
On summer afternoons did I spend grazing in the front field
Or affecting to graze?
As much as grazing, I was glutting my eyes
On my lady as she crossed her knees in her deckchair
On the flagstones between whose chasms
Aaron's Rod had seeded itself and I could see
How she exulted in Aaron's Rod – how obviously
Aaron's Rod was her pin-up wildflower, her exalted one,
All powdery nine feet of it erect but flexible
And tipped with a golden foreskin,
Its gold wattles stammering in a Mesopotamian breeze.

Suddenly she'd look up from her paperback book –
A Penguin Classic, *Thirst for Love*, Yukio Mishima –
And she'd squint up at Aaron's Rod
With such – such discreet passion
Before twirling airborne to her tiny feet
(For which no shoe shops supplied shoes so small),
And darting out two or three fingers like lizard-tongues
And curling these around the tip of the flower –
Grasping between her fingers Aaron's Rod,
Not crushing but flexing its suede texture.

I'd cease grazing, I'd cease chewing.
I'd gaze at her gazing at Aaron's Rod
And I'd go wobbly at the hocks and my superstructure
Would commence to flow, pouring forth itself

Both from my mandibles and from my hindquarters.
Lady, if you have a religion, a God,
Is it not your worship of, your cultivation of, your
    devotion to
Aaron's Rod?

The Lamb in the Oven

Unreal jealous I am of the lamb
In the Aga – in the bottom
Left-hand oven, a black lamb
On the brink of extinction,
Less than a day old, having
Its existence retrieved by you, Lady
Of the First Snowdrops and the Last Daffodils.

All day you kneel by the Aga
Resuscitating a lamb in a cardboard box,
Feeding it through a straw and
The teat of a baby's milk bottle;
Its own mother – a muddied ewe,
Marooned by a snowstorm –
Could find no way to feed her lamb.

At the kitchen window my charcoal jowls
Peeping in, grinding their molars;
Unable to comprehend that feminine
Equals maternal and that you in your rancid,
Brown cords are of all women the most feminine;
Your girl's face on your forty-odd-years-old neck.
At the windowpane of jealousy I woo you, Lady
Of the First Snowdrops and the Last Daffodils.

Lady with Portable Electric Fence

Forty-odd years old, but yet a blooming girl
On the verges of new lives leafing,
As you pace the front field
With your portable electric fence and I trumpet
Cheekily: "I am a bullock
Who worships his mistress with dung"
And I fumble in my dewlap as it wags
And unearth my antique Okinawa automatic camera
With which I have photographed you so many thousands –
No, millions – of times
In every inconceivable position in the front field.
Unique albums, but what price
The fidelity-embossed frontispiece?
A cow photographing his mistress as she bends low to
          switch on her portable electric fence.

Beijing

Dear Bansha,
I am not afraid to
Cry of love
To you although you spurn
My prancing.
O there'll be fireworks in Beijing tonight,
Fireworks in Beijing.

Dear Bansha,
Why do you disparage
Marriage?
Do you perceive fidelity
As servility?
O there'll be fireworks in Beijing tonight,
Fireworks in Beijing.

Dear Bansha,
When it came
To the cultural,
How brutal
Your commune!
O there'll be fireworks in Beijing tonight,
Fireworks in Beijing.

Dear Bansha,
No, it was not a
Skirmish we had,
Not an affair.
It was a Third World War.

O there'll be fireworks in Beijing tonight,
Fireworks in Beijing.

Dear Bansha,
Under the peaches of the
Night the route it is short
But the walk it is long
From Bansha to Beijing.
O there'll be fireworks in Beijing tonight,
Fireworks in Beijing.

The Cotoneaster of Hymenstown

In her orange denim windcheater
On a black afternoon
Lit up by a low long sun
In Dublin in November
In the doorway of my den,
She told me that she did not love me
But that she did not dislike me;
And she gave me the peck of acquaintanceship
Instead of the kiss of love.

In my little redbrick cul-de-sac
She did a U-turn.
I, swirling in my doorway,
Saluted farewell, closed the door,
Stumbled back in, sat down,
Slumped into a sideways doze
On my threadbare divan-for-two;
For she gave me the peck of acquaintanceship
Instead of the kiss of love.

Drake head down deep
In canal water in breeze,
Skinny hind legs up in the air;
I am head over heels in –
O how I fear that word –
With the Cotoneaster of Hymenstown
In her orange denim windcheater;
For she gave me the peck of acquaintanceship
Instead of the kiss of love.

Aren't you going to throw that dumb drake a crumb?
Aren't you going to throw that dumb drake a crumb?
Aren't you going to throw that dumb dake a crumb?
When he brings his heels back down and lifts up his glossy
blue skull.

Shuttlecock Made in Ireland

I

Zipping and unzipping his luggage in the lobby
     Of the Holiday Inn in Cairo –
His turquoise Samsonite overnighter –
Perspiring and itching, consistently mistaking
     His peppermints for his condoms,
His condoms for his peppermints,
He is a man – at least he thinks
     He is a man –
Who cannot stop *feeling* – "if only
     I could *think*" he thinks –
But as things lie knocked about
     Like pyramids in the desert
He is consistently mistaking
     One part of the Bible
For another part of the Bible,
     The Pharaoh for Ruth,
Ruth for the Pharaoh;
     Jerusalem for Cairo,
Cairo for Jerusalem;
     Compassion for contempt,
Contempt for compassion.

II

"That was the day she turned my condom
     Inside out and I forgot
To suck my peppermint,
     And life could never

Be the same again. Briskly
    She gleaned me,
Crisply she taught me:
    A used condom is not a death forever.
Man is man."
    Man, be glad to be man.
So help me God.

Chewing the Cud in the Lower Paddock

Chewing the cud in the Lower Paddock
On a winter's afternoon in Tipperary
I sink down to my knees in the mud,
Gasping to lay down also my head
In mud's breast and to rub
My nose in its glinting coin.
Not the done thing. Instead,
I toss back my head
Glancing up at your profile,
As in burgundy wellington boots
You stride past ignoring my fire,
Not returning my glance,
Your hands deep in the pockets
Of your belted blue gaberdine coat.

My soul is the soul of the beast;
Without you, I can know no rest.

Do I rumble at you? Naturally I rumble at you.
How could I not?
I love you, therefore I rumble at you;
For your refusal, not of myself only
But for your refusal merely to acknowledge
My being, my actual existence;
My cattleness, my jumpsuit,
My lopsidedness, my big ears,
My gauche toilette,
My carnal spirituality;

Your refusal to look at me – to give me
So much as one second of your time;
Your chariness of my parts;
Your indifference to my haunches.

My soul is the soul of the beast;
Without you, I can know no rest.

The Cattle Dealer's Daughter

Daughter of the Island Fields, what
Must we do to alert you
As we muck about in our dying?
We cattle – we machines of death?

You will eat us and that
Will be that, but what we'd like
Is for you to know also our outsides
As well as our insides.

There you are once again hanging out
On the banks watching the two rivers in flood.
What we'd like is a slice of eye-contact,
If not an uncut cake of it.

After you're gone and it's twilight –
Zero black, zero wet, zero cold –
What I regret is your not looking
Into the milky bogholes of my eyes.

Will you look ever into my eyes?
Lay your hand ever on my brow?
So that, kicking out my hooves, I can low:
"She said nothing, but she gave me her hand."

Daughter of the Island Fields, what
Is it about us that you treat us
Like bodiless spirits – we cattle
Chained to our weeping tails?

Out of lamplit silence you stroll,
Back into lamplit silence you glide,
While we in our nights go on dying:
Depleting, depleting, depleting.

My Bride of Aherlow

Oh was it that in my black book sack
I carried too many years?
And that the hairs of my head were grey
And gelled in too many tears?
That in the cave pools of my eyes
There was not a goldfish to arouse?
That down the arches of my eyes
Streeled ivy of brows?
O marry me now in my grave, my grave,
My Bride of Aherlow!

Or was it that in my black book sack
There were no seeds to be seen?
Or only such seeds as were too scarce
To sow in a pink tureen?
That for every bead of silver seed
There were too many sheaths of dust?
Or blacker than dust or polythene
An odour of things unseen?
O marry me now in my grave, my grave,
My Bride of Aherlow!

Or was it that in my black book sack
I carried near nothing at all?
Not even food for the table,
Nor drink for the long black haul?
Was it that all I could claim my own
Was the road and the sky and the night?

That my ears were pricked and my nostrils dilated
To a premonition of fright?
O marry me now in my grave, my grave,
My Bride of Aherlow.

Or was it in fact that the actual sack –
The actual Mayo black book sack –
Had nothing in it at all?
That when you delved down dark and deep,
Laughingly hopefully down dark deep,
There was Mars-like nothing there;
Nothing that God or woman could save
Or knead up a thorny stair?
O marry me now in my grave, my grave,
My Bride of Aherlow.

Tulip

Nosing through the rubbish skip
        at the T-junction
I sniff her white cotton nightgown
        and turn it up
From among lids of washing machines
        and broken drums.

I chew it at my leisure
        sleeve by sleeve;
With patience and expectation
        devour it;
Its crotchetwork
        obstructing me to nibbles.

I who with my tail
        high above four legs
Am the green-eyed
        gourmet of her soul:
Gourmet of all
        that is,
Was, ever will be
        Straw!

In the Valley near Slievenamon

"Tulip!" you peal. "Tulip!"
I glance up from my grazing, gazing at you
As you ride astride the five-barred gate
Freshening up your lips with a tube of lipstick,
Pursing them. Oh, when you purse,
I flick my tail, swishing it
In hopes to retrieve the kiss of love I've forfeited.

You jump down and, hitching up your denim skirt,
You squat down on haunches under whitethorn;
Answering, as you call it, "the call of nature",
A woman watering her father's grass;
Confiding in me that nobody is looking!
As if I am nobody! Cow-content to be nobody

Sufferably I experience a surge of affinity –
Consanguinity of my cowsoul with your
      womanflesh –
And summoning up all my bowels and all my bladders
And holding high all my jowls
I bring down antique gold velvet curtains of urine –
Quilts of fire –
Succeeded by sedate descents of poxy pizzas.

For you prided yourself on being a candid woman
Who always left the bathroom door wide open,
As if to highlight our common regeneration –
A sweet defiance of all darkness and all shame –

And, in a sunbeam unbunged by God,
Not to deny the divinity of dung.

Cowlady in bloodgreased second-hand green anorak
In the valley near Slievenamon!

Fethard

In Fethard I could not wear your anger
That night my hooves trampled your roses:
"My mistake," I pleaded – "my mistake."

Prowling in Fethard this afternoon in the rain
You are trying to find a space to park your car.
Dear – you may park your car in *my* roses!

Your 1956 bottlegreen Jaguar in Fethard,
All mahogany dashboard and red leather:
Can you not smell my blood upon your bonnet?

Animals Who Meet on the Road

Four miles outside town
On the main road,
I among the herd shuffling
Between hedgerows, swaying
My loaded hulk, lolling
My head, when she
On the motorbike appears
On the crest of the bend,
Changes down the gears,
Her son's red-and-black
Honda 50 cc,
Slowing to a standstill
In the middle of the road,
Awaiting us to flow
Past either side of her.

I manoeuvre myself
Into the midstream that will
Canoe me closest to her.
I peer into her eyes,
Her visor up,
But there is not an ember
Of recognition in her eyes.
In my confinement I squeak.
Is it that she cannot hear
Or that she will not hear?
In my plush flanks I brush
Up against her thighs –
Bedenimed blue stretched back

To the white seam of her crotch.
I detect her flutter to my brush –
A clean elation.
I can perceive her psyche impinge brighter,
But mine putting on weight
By the udderful of melancholia.

What is it in a spirited woman
That renders her so impatient
With her man or bullock
That she must accelerate
Onto the next man, the next bullock?
That rather than cultivate
She would speculate?
Brandishing her gauntlets,
She revolves her wrists, revs
Her conniving machine,
Its obsequious chrome,
Dives off downhill
Into the county town.

The Lady Testifies

"Testicle" – that is a vocable
When the lady testifies
She revels in, especially the plural of –
"Testicles". Or the adjectival "testicular".

If I exhibit an inkling of flinching
She reproaches me – "Why not?
Men are forever reverberating on their tongues
'Breast' or 'breasts'."

She reiterates the word with relish
"Testicle" or "testicles";
Gravely she'll say:
"I'm not sure that you're environmentally testicular."

I feel so self-conscious I can no longer stand
In the front field at evening in profile
Without feeling that her eyes
Are trained on my rod –

My abrupt rod
Hanging down hopelessly in a steely north-easterly,
Its hairy goosepimples focussed
In her Swiss binoculars.

Tonight – a pink summer's night –
I can stand it no more.
I potshot at her, ricocheting:
"I am not my testicles".

But the lady continues to testify:
"You are nothing else but your testicles.
Whereas, upstairs, I with my bloody cranesbill breasts
Am downstairs so much more than my bloody cranesbill
    breasts."

On the Brink of Her Ecstasy,
He Collapses

On the brink of her ecstasy, he collapses
And she reads him the riot act for the last time:
The 1439 Act for the Encouragement of Joy in Females.
At 3 a.m. in her despair, she probes him:

"Tulip, O Tulip,
Why do you, as the male, always assume
That I, as the woman, know everything?
Don't you know yet after all these zillennia
That a woman is not omniscient,
Although most of the time she has to pretend to be
And, in the agribusiness of the bed, all of the time?

"When will you ever learn that Iran is not Iraq?
That the Hebrides are not the Orkneys?
That Mayo is not Mayo?
That in Brazil we do not speak Spanish?
Dear man – for dear you are, although not belovèd –
Your knowledge of geography below a woman's waist
Is about as dependable as your knowledge of the
    Netherlands.

"Why always are you all fingers and no thumbs?
On the other hand or, I should say,
And say acutely, on the other breast,
You take it for granted that I,
As the earth-goddess with my watering cans and
    my hoses,

Should know all about the vagaries of your wildflower –
All the highs and lows of your pink, black rod!

"I am weary O so weary
Of all the responsibility always being laid on me.
Stop mistaking me for a mother bear in a golden forest
When it is I who live in the real cave,
The life of the real bat, hanging upside-down
In all my crevices, my nooks, my chasms.
O thumb my upsidedownness with your two thumbs
Or away with you and your butter-fingers, back to your
    bimbo heifers.
It is three o'clock in the morning, go to sleep."

Valentine's Day

Wake at eight elated.
Herbal tea and toast and
Go back to manger and wait
For postman to come
And make his drop –
That devout thud
Of post upon cave floor.

Dozing, sonogram it, sidle
Out of manger, peer
Down bannister, cannot
Credit it. Instead
Of grove of snowdrops and crocuses,
One off-brown cellophane-windowed
Envelope on floor.
Hurtle downstairs to find
It's a *Time* magazine reminder
To pay up a subscription
I've never asked for.

Clinging on to wall in hall,
Clutching pyjama bottoms,
In which elastic has gone,
I sink to my hocks, curdling
My tears with my urine.
In my father's mansion
On the Feast of Saint Valentine
What a mess I am in!

In the Days before Milking Parlours
and Mobile Phones

In the days before milking parlours and mobile phones
And you were a mountain woman how radically
You used to skip across the courtyard –
Polishing its cobblestones in your steel slippers –
With a milkpail in one arm and a three-legged stool!

A virtuoso xylophonist would have envied
Your fingers as they played me –
Making music on the tin scree of the pail –
As you leaned your head into my sirloins;
As your brain mushroomed with my blood!

I doze being stared at by your dead lonely father
While you in your *Au Bon Marché* red-and-blue frock
On the arm of your new beau
Attend the world première of *The End of the Affair*
In the Savoy cinema opposite the G.P.O.

In the days before milking parlours and mobile phones
And you were a mountain woman, how radically
You believed in domestic peace and romantic fidelity;
In faith, hope, and charity in the mean streets
Jigsawing down to the river and the G.P.O.

I arise to my hooves in a crux, and bawl out my bifocals!

29 February

Dozing in day-moon
With my cranium in my knees,
I muse on you the far
Side of the river
In your open-plan, decapitating
Tipperary sparkling water.

"Blood is thicker than water,"
You insist. O yes,
It is, but is
Blood thicker than seed?

How many times did we make love
Or – in your vernacular – "copulate"?
Yet today you will not cross
The river to say hmmmm
Or to give me seven seconds of your time.

Not a word from you
This leap year afternoon
Of black showers, gold breezes,
The last of the snowdrops,
The first of the daffodils.

I inch up to the iron trotters
Of the pig's feet of the Eiffel Tower
And the lone, level lawns
Of the Champ-de-Mars,

Green as black nectar
And gold with the shaved heads
Of marching souls as they salute
Adieu to their frail mates:
A woman wages all-out war on her man.

Oxtail

When you'd set down oxtail soup
Before me on the kitchen table –
Baxter's –
You'd cry: "Drink up your oxtail soup."
If I stayed dumb, making no reply,
You'd repeat it: "Drink up your oxtail soup."
If I still made no reply
You'd cry out again: "Drink up your oxtail soup."

Why was I so dejected
At the spectacle of oxtail soup?
You presumed because I am an ox
Thereby I am insulted by oxtail soup
But no – what demented me
Was the possessive pronoun in your cry:
That "*your*" – that "*your* oxtail soup".

Is there not in possessiveness
An estranging note
Which the gods abhor?
I am an ox who abhors
Oxtail soup that's *yours*.
The only grass that is good
Is the grass that is not mine
Or yours – the grass that grows
In the changing skies between our toes.
The night is not unchanging.

Bullock with Cut Head

Of the years when you pastured me in the field in front
    of the house
        I have only colourful memories.
It was only when you turned me out down into the
    lower paddock,
        Into the black and the white,
        That I repined.

To visitors or to your brothers and sisters you opined
        Of new grass and old grass
And they imbibed your Tipperary vowels with the white
    wine
        Peering out prismatic Georgian windows
        Of eighteenth-century glass.

        Out of sight out of mind,
        Under the family tree,
        In the lower paddock,
        I stand staring at blood,
        Sentinel to my death.

All right, all right; I'm going, I'm going.
        Was I to know it was the family tree?
I stood under it to get in out of the sun,
        Bleeding my foreigness.
        I'm going, I'm going.

National Cleavage Day,
30 March 2000

National Cleavage Day, 30 March 2000,
I get a packet in the post,
Recognise the knitted handwriting –
My loyal companion
In the bosom of whose affection
How many early evenings
I have lain, and late mornings!

With exhilaration of anticipation
I leave it unopened
For the day on the breakfast table.
Late in the afternoon
Over a mug of real tea
I'll stretch out my hooves,
Kick off my shoes,
Contemplate the treetops over the sheds
And utilising the sharp letter-opener
Posted me by my cousin Frank
With his name and address inscribed on it –
The auctioneer in Chapel Street –
I'll slit it open with in-your-face relish.

It contains a crumpled paperback
The Age of Walled Gardens
By Jack Whaley
With a foreword by Sir Simon Hornby
Published by the Fieldgate Press of Kells
And a scrawled note in blue Bic biro

Instructing me to find enclosed
The Christmas present
She'd forgotten to send me
And that she has to say –
As she puts it –
She has to say
It is time to call it a night.
Joke? No joke.
Goodbye Paul. With Love. Cita.

National Cleavage Day, 30 March 2000
I am left peering into the abyss.

Torn in Two

That twenty-two page love letter in which
I slopped out my heart to you,
Comparing you, my mountain woman,
With a gold hoard secreted in loughwater
Under a thorn tree in Rear Cross –
How I waited day after day for a reply,
Week after week, month after month.
When after seven months a reply came
I did not recognise your hand on the envelope
But inside there it was, my letter,
My twenty-two page love letter, all of it,
Which you had torn in two.

I am a bright man torn in two.
Have I no hope of being a union with you?
Not a eunuch – a union?
I get up every day torn in two.
I trudge over to the minimart torn in two.
I buy my sliced pan torn in two.
I buy my low-fat milk torn in two.
I traipse back home torn in two.
I crouch in front of the TV torn in two.
I gobble my microwave dinner torn in two.
I kneel down at my bed torn in two.
I whisper my bedtime prayers torn in two.
I clamber into bed torn in two.
But I cannot go to sleep torn in two.
I read about the Taliban torn in two.

I spend the night on my back torn in two.
I get up every day torn in two.
Have I no hope of being one with you?
I am a bright man torn in two.

Turbo Intercooler Mitsubishi *Pajero*

She who once was a country girl with a swerve in her stride
Walking her land in burgundy wellington boots,
Is now a cattle farmer who drives
A Turbo Intercooler Mitsubishi *Pajero*
Herding us from the high land to the low

Or delivering meals on wheels.
When she arrives at my manger
If I do not instantly rise to my hindquarters
She bangs down my plate on the sill,
Abandoning it to the flies and the midges.

Tonight in the county library she has a lecture to give
In which she will speak of the veterinary imperative
Of goading the beasts and taunting the hormones
And how even in cattle past their prime
One's bones cry out for another's bones.

While I in the night by my manger toss
Marooned on the drumlin of my carcass
In a death watch that knows no shores
Or islands until the guillotine falls
And the meatslicer divides my parts.

In dawn light she swoops up in her bull-bar
To pick up her moiety – "his private parts"
Jovially she cries – and she illustrates them
In her public lecture with slides
To the Tipperary Cattle Farmers' Association

In the Kickham Imperial Hotel and after
A feed of red wine, black stout,
She drives back to her Georgian farmhouse
In her Turbo Intercooler Mitsubishi *Pajero*
Whistling Darina Allen recipes, humming *Trailfinders*
    package holidays

In Thailand with her new man.

Brucellosis

She'd never admit it
But I was not
Intellectual enough for her.
I'd be nosing in the river
In dumb mode
And I'd glimpse the curl
Of impatience on her lip.

I needed to bellow at her:
Woman, you don't have a clue about cattle!
In my four hooves, snout, tail
My soul has known it all and retro-rocketed
Out beyond intellect
Into the actuality of the cosmos.

Does it never occur to you,
Woman of the Black Cow,
That a man has a body?
That sometimes even I –
A gregarious hermit of the meadow –
Even I get so nauseated and weary
Of brucellosis and all
That brucellosis entails?
That I get so sad and sick
Of abortion after abortion,
I curse the deity why O why
This habitual, this contagious
Abortion after abortion?
Woman, climb down

Off your high horse of intellect,
Your arctic mare of beauty,
All that gear and tackle
Of black leather language,
All that Bollocky Bill.

O lie down with me in my stained straw
And in the stable of habitual abortion
Divine the reality of the flesh –
What it means to be a cow like me,
What it means to live in your body.
Brucellosis also is part of the process of the stars.

Desert Island Bull

I

Caressing my hide with her voice
She selected me to be
Her desert island bull.

Like a young mother giving birth,
The helicopter pilot winched me down
Onto the hotplate shore.

She had it all organised;
Me all to herself,
Me all between her knees.

Of all the desert bulls
In the island of Ireland
No bull was more contented

Than I in her breasts
Or, as I thought, belovèd.
Grass, sand, and water!

Next morning was brilliant.
Her Ray-Bans high up in her hair,
She on her mobile.

Without a "Ciao" she sauntered
Away from me and I howled
Under the rotor blades lifting off.

II

I try to forget you, but I cannot forget you.
At dawn every day I see you frolicking in your bathroom
With your new beau hanging out of your kneecaps.
I understand that to you, Woman of the Black Cow,
I am but a bull and no more than a bull,
A machine with a finite number of programmes.
You've selected a new bull, a new desert island.
They say it's one of the 365 islands of Clew Bay;
That your new bull's a New Jerseyite who wears his
    skipping ropes
Around his neck. The curse of Bofin on you both.
May his skipping ropes self-destruct in your sarongs.
May you choke on his tail.
May both your carcasses be washed up in a fifth-hand
    bicycle knacker's yard in a back street off the Castlebar
    road in Ballyhaunis.

Slobbering at Lughnasa

Silhouetted on the skyline at noon –
After a change of fields at dawn,
New grass floating on a lagoon of dew –
I am standing ears-equal to all aerials,
Masts and dishes:
I am riding at anchor
In the fullness of my four stomachs.

Monarch of the Glen of Aherlow,
High King of all I survey
Until I behold her spiralling up the fields
Through high corn splashed with poppies
And catching that conceited, girly glance of hers,
I appreciate that she cannot help but feel
Colonial superiority over me,
Her Celtic slob.
I am suffused with a subversive pity for her
And for all of her species that they have forgotten
That males also are beasts of the field;
That her existence also if she but knew it –
Peeled to its essence –
Is but a digestive process.
But – skewing her hips at me
She chooses not to hear my cow-consonants
And I hover there before her slobbering
And that's all she hears, that's all she sees,
Poor girl.

The Girl from Golden

I could endure your anger
When you'd produce your ashplant
To beat the buttocks off me, breezily
Chanting your rural middleclass chant.

But what I cannot endure
Is your curt, omnipotent, inexplicable fatwa
That I be ostracised, ignored, and never again granted
Anything but the brunt of your indifference.

Under the river-reflecting boughs of a leafing chestnut
I gape at all that night flowing underneath me
With its flintstones for galaxies
And its one solitary conger eel for a milky way.

SMILING COW FOUND DROWNED IN RIVER SUIR

I wouldn't be the first smiling cow to commit suicide
Because of a Girl from Golden.

Lady of the Golden Vale

But now that you have planted me out
     to the last paddocks of autumn –
Conway's Field on the Bansha road –
     and I am in the autumn of my years
Why is it that when you drive the land
     you cannot afford to dispense me
So much as a syllable of a charitable word?
     Why even in early morning
Is your spiky shell so hardcased against me?

When I glimpse you driving out from beneath
     The saffron grove –
The lime tree fattening its thighs to your satisfaction –
The horse chestnut dangling pithy shells for you to split –
Your esteemed crows flying with apples in their beaks –
     My legs – my four legs –
All of them quivering at the knees with anticipation
     Of a flicker of a smile
     From the lockets of your eyes;
Of an unconditional amnesty;
     Of a clear-eyed oblivion;
Of a cousinly forgiveness of all family secrets;
Of an inexplicable absolution of impossible existence.

So when, from the driving seat of your four-wheel drive,
     You ambush me with a broken bottle
Of assessment, a second broken bottle
     Of adjudication (and you
The most beautiful lady of Tipperary)

I am taken – taken
Wholly by surprise and down again.

O Lady of the Golden Vale all those years ago
   At the Kilfinnane Fair
Was I the obtusest cow of all to go
   Far away off home with you
In the summer of my years?
   "He was some Tulip!"
I hear is what you shriek or murmur
To your coffee-for-schizophrenia friends:
   "He was some Tulip!"

The Camaraderie of the Mart

Modelling my live meat in the cattle mart
I spot her at the same time as I hear her voice:
That haughty blarney blaring out its conceit –
"O don't you love the camaraderie of the mart?"

On tenterhooks of hooves I prance the ramp,
Not knowing if she will champion me or deny me;
Her waistlong hair tied up in a burgundy scrunchie;
Burgundy chiffon scarf to match each burgundy wellie.

With ashplant stick she leans out and switches me
On rump and shoulders. I eye her yodel:
"Have you ever seen the likes of such shoulders?"
Mute, rhinoceros-nostrilled her sister farmers scowl.

She repeats and I repeat and they repeat
That all that counts with them is my dead meat.
For the beauty of my soul they do not give a
        couturier's —— :
"O don't you love the camaraderie of the mart?"

Bovril

At all hours of the night
I am to be periscoped sleepwalking
The half-moon of the top field,
Booming at the top of my hindquarters:
But why did she ditch me?
At around noon I like to get up
And before breakfast have a dribble.
Between 2 and 3 p.m.
I slurp my Bovril.

Was it Bovril that did for me?
Yes I think it was Bovril that did for me.
That and the fact that her father also was a Bovril
    drinker.
Now that I brood on it
Did she not browbeat me one day:
"You must choose between Bovril and me"?
I – assuming she was teasing –
Snorted in her face and lowed
"Bovril forever and forever Bovril".
After that she never faxed me again.

Her new beau quaffs beer, pints of it.
God, he looks so deficient
In the lounge bar with his back to the door
In his cushy combats quaffing pints of beer!
Whereas here am I out here in the raw nude
On the side of a mountain slurping my Bovril.

Bananas

All night alone between stone walls,
Elongated in a concupiscent trance,
After having parleyed with the lady for three hours
Snout to snout at the brass rail
And lowing goodnight overheard her say –
I who always take the worst for granted –
Her say "When will I see you again?"
And she pinched a T-bone
And posied her fingers on my nose.

First thing at noon I roly-poly uphill to her half-door.
She opens her half-door with not a smear of a smile
And I am taken aback – sidefooted
By her – what should I call it? – her *hypothermia*.
She proffers me a banana and she sighs:
I can only offer you bananas.
For the umpteenth muckout, I am taken by surprise
Not by my bovinity
With which I am by millennia ossified
But by the collosal naïveté of my bovinity.
The naïveté of cattle is known only to the fifty-fifth
    eyelash of Queen Elizabeth the First.

The White Ox of Foxbrook

When our ball alley dissolved into desuetude
At the end of the 1950's,
Our parish priest, in order to preserve it,
Built the new ballroom around the old ball alley,
"Mating" – as from the pulpit he seduced us –
"Two edifices in the one romance."
The old ball alley would be a feature of the new
       ballroom.

May I have the pleasure of the next dance?
No.
Would you like a Babycham in the Ball Alley?
Maybe.

That was forty years ago.
The ballroom of romance fell down.
Our beloved parish priest let it be known
That a jiving lady had glanced down at her
       gentleman's feet
And espied a pair of cloven hooves.

The ball alley again is open to the skies –
To cattle cries:
The ball alley is trimmed around by broken glass
And strips of dance floor that haven't yet
Been car-booted away for firewood.

I am the White Ox of Foxbrook
In the ball alley on a summer's evening
Ballooning keens:

Every part of me's bleeding,
Where does the holy water come from?

The Price of Gas

Was it when you read the news
That the European Union
Had announced new quotas
On Ireland's greenhouse
Gas emissions,
Relating uniquely
To the flatulence of cattle –
To our passing wind –
Or, as the EU
Legislation terms it,
"The gut process methane gas
Of the enteric fermentation
In ruminant animals,"
That led you in August
That humid morn
To ditch me
And to fax me
Your terminal endearment
Ciao Malodorous
Which came in a second time
Malodorous Ciao?

All that humid morning
My fax kept on repeating:
Ciao Malodorous
Malodorous Ciao.

I am a sore, sad, sick cow
That would like to gore her fax.
Cita – can you hear me? –
May I gore your fax?

Abattoir

Although in the abattoir it is her red rubber-gloved hand
That first I see upon the lever –
She for whom I have lived my double life
In the river fields with such passivity –
She for whom I would forever low
Or abstain from grass if she expressed the wish –
Although I know that that hand of hers,
Too mottled for hate, yet tautly freckled,
Will pull that lever and annex my fate,
It is to her lips that I yet appeal,
Raising my hairy eyes to equal her gaze.
O lady love you are not fated to guillotine me:
In the vast, black emptiness of the abattoir
I clap my lips with your lips, abstemiously.

Forgetting the Ox

Her life as a woman
Is a thirty-year story
Of learning how to forget;
She who was idolised
By the ox of her eye
Replies to his ox-love
With balletic neglect.

When she encounters me
On the road and I stare
In disbelief's grief
Into her ox-forgetting eyes
She smiles as she says:
I disremember you, ox.

My life as an ox
Was a life of folly
But also of charity.
She murmurs: I disdain you
Because you love me –
Those curse-of-God, poetry-scribbling hooves.

On the last lorry ride to the slaughterhouse
Glimpsing her through the slats I perceive
That all that fascinates her about her ox
Is his slaughter. Unfurling her moneybelt
She smiles meteorically:
"Ladylife in Ireland in the 2000s
Is all about forgetting the ox."

Easter Sunday

That Easter Sunday midnight Mass under a gold moon
When we circled side by side outside the village church
Around the Paschal Fire, and peace doves were uncaged,
The bullet of your need pierced my hide.
I detected it zigzagging, hovering, percolating,
Re-entering me like a philanthropic ricochet
And orbiting round my stomachs and my bowel
Like a homing Sputnik relieved to home
Into the dung-bejewelled tabernacle of my soul.
The priest intoned: "Do you renounce
The devil and his works?" "I do,"
I mooed exuberantly in the ultramarine night
And the Great Lakes of your eyes – Superior and Erie –
Spumed up out of your lips in their floral wreaths.

A Little Woman

Than whom there is no gentler, fiercer
Spirit; no sweeter, crueller nature; no more
Forgiving, merciless mate; no keener breeder
Not only of cattle but of turkeys too.
Would I have had more chance with you
Had I been a turkey, not a cow?
In the turkey sheds in the yew trees
At plucking time in Advent in December,
Among batteries of identical-looking turkeys
Would you have picked me out, wed me to the bone?
Not for my petty cash but for myself alone?
Or would a good little woman such as you
Be no more faithful to a turkey than to a cow?
Dung, feathers, for your fire, in Christmas snow.

Fear is the Prong

Never did affection circulate so freely
Between two creatures and yet it was I
As your stud bull who was always fearful of you –
The forty-odd-year-old young girl in her prime
Of femininity, her tenderness.
Knowing that if even for a few seconds
I failed to concentrate and allowed
My horned udder to float about in the clouds
And I inclined to print a stray hoof
In your herbaceous border, you would chase me
With a three-pronged pitchfork, not necessarily
In jest, more probably in earnest,
And, as we flailed the buttercup acres,
If you could not catch up with me
You'd become a minuscule maquette of a javelin thrower
Hurling your pitchfork after me,
Either plucking my hindquarters, making me hop along
With pain, or finding only lush, tidal grass
From which to retrieve a pitchfork's drowned prong.

The Second Coming

All that the infant child can know –
That Infant Child is seeming to say –
Is that the cow is innately good;
Homo sapiens may – may not be – good
But not innately – no way innately.

The infant child is more at home with the cow,
More instinctively, intuitively at home with
    the cow;
My hooves, my tongue, my ears, my tail.
The infant child comprehends what it is
That keeps me going on head down:

Precisely what it is that motivates me
To adorn and endure the vales of Tipperary.
The cow is the palpitating embodiment
Of day-to-day faith in the Second Coming:
I am the personification of innocence.

How could a cow not believe in the Second
    Coming?
The Second Coming is what gets me up out of it
    off my knees.
It is what holds me together,
All my parts, my rivets, my cross-struts;
All my floppy berets, all my trailing scarves.

At every Bethlehem you will always find me
In the second row manuring the straw,

Extraterrestrial eyebrows in exuberant excelsis;
The black-and-white cow of the Parousia
Licking the ears of the Mother of God.

A Day in the Cave

Getting up in the morning is hardest.
I detest getting up. But I do. I usedn't to.
The first five hours are the worst.
But around 12.30 bits of light
Squirrel about on my wall
And I begin to get ideas –
Maybe Cita will call.

Of course there is no way
Cita will call
But that's not the point.
I imagine her calling and that's it –
I'm away – I'm tidying up –
Out with the *Windowlene* and the *Ajax*,
The *Harpic* and the *Dettol* –
Combing my hair, straightening my collar –
Booming about the cave –
Cita! Cita!
Delighted to see you, Cita! –
Banging up against the walls of the cave.

No, it's not only that I suffer from an affliction
Labelled inconsolable loneliness, which I do –
It's that there's not many a woman like her
In the parish of the world.
She's all hips and intellect – the broad hips
Of the kind of traveller woman who supports
A community of ten caravans – the intricate brain
Of a research wizard in immunology.

Christ, what's that?
A tapping at the door.
It must be her after all, Jesus
All Merciful!
I jump up. Fling this notebook under the table –
This black Capital Finesse 320-page spiral notebook
That I always get in *Reads* of Nassau Street –
Glance at myself in the mirror.
Steady myself like a pole-vaulter
    Getting ready to approach
        The run-up to the ultimate
            Vault – the vault that
                Will see him over the edge
                    Of this parish into the next,
                        Muttering a mantra:
O let there be an end to politically-correct, sectarian,
    nouveau riche, low-skies-infested Ireland!

I snap open the door and behold
Nobody standing there, nobody,
And I peer out hoping
To find her locking her door.
What kind of car has she?
Yes, a metallic grey *Fiesta*, that's it!
From out behind a metallic grey *Fiesta*
Peeps Sabrina, my neighbour,
My four-year-old neighbour:
"Have you any sweets, Paul?"

Paul – in the door of his cave pawing air.